Bond

STRETCH
Maths
Tests and Papers

10–11+ years

Paul Broadbent

Text © Paul Broadbent 2012
Original illustrations © Nelson Thornes Ltd 2012

The right of Paul Broadbent to be identified as author of this work has been asserted by him in accordance with the Copyright, Designs and Patents Act 1988.

All rights reserved. No part of this publication may be reproduced or transmitted in any form or by any means, electronic or mechanical, including photocopy, recording or any information storage and retrieval system, without permission in writing from the publisher or under licence from the Copyright Licensing Agency Limited, of Saffron House, 6–10 Kirby Street, London, EC1N 8TS.

Any person who commits any unauthorised act in relation to this publication may be liable to criminal prosecution and civil claims for damages.

Published in 2012 by:

Nelson Thornes Ltd
Delta Place
27 Bath Road
CHELTENHAM
GL53 7TH
United Kingdom

12 13 14 15 16 / 10 9 8 7 6 5 4 3 2 1

A catalogue record for this book is available from the British Library

ISBN 978 14085 1868 7

Page make-up and illustrations by GreenGate Publishing Services, Tonbridge, Kent

Printed and bound in Spain by GraphyCems

Introduction

What is Bond?

The Bond Stretch series is a new addition to the Bond range of Assessment papers, the number one series for the 11+, selective exams and general practice. Bond Stretch is carefully designed to challenge above and beyond the level provided in the regular Bond assessment range.

How does this book work?

The book contains two distinct sets of papers, along with full answers and a Progress Chart:

- Focus tests, accompanied by advice and directions, which are focused on particular (and age-appropriate) Maths question types encountered in the 11+ and other exams, but devised at a higher level than the standard Assessment papers. Each focus test is designed to help raise a child's skills in the question type as well as offer plenty of practice for the necessary techniques.

- Mixed papers, which are full-length tests containing a full range of Maths question types. These are designed to provide rigorous practice for children working at a level higher than that required to pass at the 11+ and other Maths tests.

- Full answers are provided for both types of test in the middle of the book.

- At the back of the book, there is a Progress Chart which allows you to track your child's progress.

- Some questions may require a ruler or a protractor. Calculators are not permitted.

How much time should the tests take?

The tests are for practice and to reinforce learning, and you may wish to test exam techniques and working to a set time limit. We would recommend your child spends 50 minutes to answer the 50 questions in each Mixed paper. You can reduce the suggested time by five minutes to practise working at speed.

Using the Progress Chart

The Progress Chart can be used to track Focus test and Mixed paper results over time to monitor how well your child is doing and identify any repeated problems in tackling the different question types.

Focus test 1 — Place value

When you compare, order and round whole numbers and decimals, look carefully at the value of each digit.

1 Write the heights of these mountains in order, starting with the highest.

Mountain	Height (feet)
Jannu	25299
Kamet	25446
Lhotse	27940
Makalu	27838
Nuptse	25801

Mountain	Height (feet)

Use these four digits and the decimal point to answer both these questions. There is one digit in front of the decimal point in each answer.

7   3   4   8   .

2 What is the largest possible decimal number you can make?   __ . __ __ __

3 What is the decimal number that is as near as possible to 4?   __ . __ __ __

Round each of these measurements to the nearest tenth.

4 12.75 cm _____   5 34.63 m _____   6 5.908 kg _____

Write the missing numbers in these calculations. Choose from 10, 100 or 1000.

7 46.93 ÷ __ = 4.693   8 807.9 × __ = 807900   9 375.4 ÷ __ = 3.754

10 What is the value of the digit 5 in the number 23.056? _____

11 3.09 × 1000 = _____

12 I'm thinking of a number less than 1. The two digits total 9 and it rounds to 0.6 to the nearest tenth. What number is it? 0. __ __

Now go to the Progress Chart to record your score!   Total   12

Focus test 2 — Multiplication and division

If numbers are too large to multiply or divide mentally, use a written method and always estimate an approximate answer first.

1 Complete this multiplication grid.

×	7	12	30
9			
		96	
11	77		

2
```
   238
 ×  36
```

Example:
```
   167
 ×  53
   501    (167 × 3)
  8350    (167 × 50)
  8851
```

_____

3 What is 435 × 74?

×	400	30	5
70			
4			

Total: _____

Example: What is 236 × 23?

×	200	30	6	
20	4000	600	120	4720
3	600	90	18	708

Total: 5428

4 Circle the division that has a remainder of 3.

239 ÷ 7   548 ÷ 4   614 ÷ 9   307 ÷ 8

5 Write the missing digits.

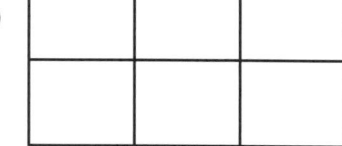

5

6 This length of ribbon is divided into four equal lengths. How long is each length? _____

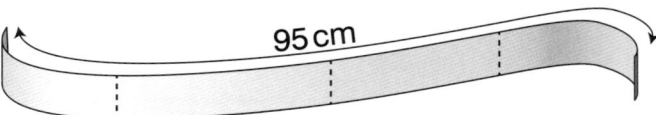

7 What is the area of a square with sides of 2.5 cm?

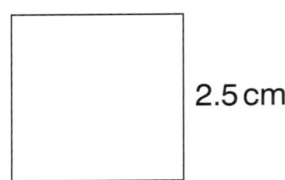

2.5 cm

Area = _____

8 £573 is divided equally between four people.

How much do they each get? _____

9 Three identical books have a total weight of 2400 g.

What is the weight of five of these books? _____

10 A farmer collects 134 eggs and puts them into egg boxes that each holds 6 eggs.

How many egg boxes will he fill? _____

11 Alex saved £9.50 a week for 25 weeks.

How much has he saved altogether? _____

12 A lorry holds 1589 kg of sugar. It is divided equally into five containers.

How much sugar is in each container? _____

Now go to the Progress Chart to record your score! Total 12

Focus test 3 — Factors, multiples and prime numbers

> Prime numbers only have two factors, 1 and itself. The number 1 is not a prime number as it only has one factor.

1. Write the missing factors for 72.

   (1, __) (__, __) (__, __) (__, __) (__, __) (__, __)

2. Write the numbers 3, 4, 6 and 9 to complete these.

   184 is a multiple of ____.

   243 is a multiple of ____ and ____.

   276 is a multiple of ____, ____ and ____.

3. Write these numbers on the Venn diagram.

   20   35   8   45   30   21   4

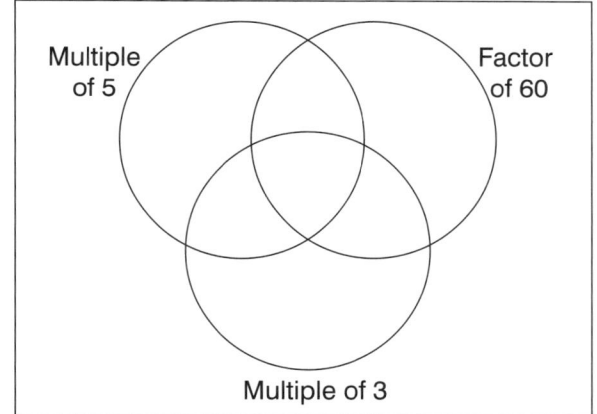

4. Here are all the pairs of factors for a number. Write the number and complete the missing factors.

   ____ → (1, __) (2, __) (3, __) (4, 12) (6, __)

5. The lowest common multiple of 6 and 8 is 24.

   What is the lowest common multiple of these pairs of numbers?

   9 and 8 ____   5 and 4 ____   4 and 6 ____

The numbers 1, 2, 3 and 6 are common factors of 24 and 18.
The highest common factor (HCF) of 24 and 18 is 6.
List the common factors and circle the HCF for each of these sets of numbers.

6 Common factors of 72 and 48: _____

7 Common factors of 45, 36 and 90: _____

8 Which two factors of 144 have a total of 30? ____ and ____

9 Choose any of these prime numbers to complete the multiplications:

          3   5   11   17   19

__ × __ × __ = 1045   __ × __ × __ = 561

10 Which three consecutive prime numbers multiply to make 385?

__ × __ × __ = 385

11 What are the factors of the square numbers 4, 9 and 16?

   4 _____   9 _____   16 _____

12 What do you notice about the factors of any square number?

_____

_____

Now go to the Progress Chart to record your score!   Total   12

Focus test 4 — Fractions, decimals, percentages, ratios and proportions

To compare fractions with different denominators, change them to equivalent fractions with a common denominator.

Look at these number cards.

[3] [5] [2] [9]

Use two of the cards to complete these. 1 $\dfrac{\square}{\square} < \dfrac{1}{2}$ 2 $\dfrac{\square}{\square} = 0.6$

3 These are Sam's maths test scores as marks out of a total.

Convert each of the scores to a percentage.

37 out of 50 = _____   18 out of 20 = _____   21 out of 25 = _____

4 What is the ratio of grey tiles to white tiles? _____

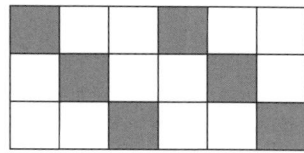

5 How many white tiles are needed if 90 tiles are used in this pattern?

_____

6 Write the missing digits to complete these.

$\dfrac{1}{\square} = 0.\square = 20\%$ $\dfrac{\square}{4} = 0.75 = \square\%$ $\dfrac{1}{20} = 0.\square = \square\%$

7 Write these fractions in order, starting with the smallest.

$\dfrac{1}{2}$ $\dfrac{3}{4}$ $\dfrac{2}{5}$ $\dfrac{5}{8}$

_____

8 This boat is drawn at a scale of 150∶1. The drawing is 4 cm long.

How long is the actual boat? _____

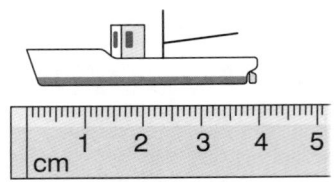

9 Sophie mixes 3 litres of white paint with every 5 litres of blue paint.

She needs 24 litres of paint altogether.

How many tins of blue paint will she need? _____

In this recipe each ingredient is given as a proportion of the total weight.

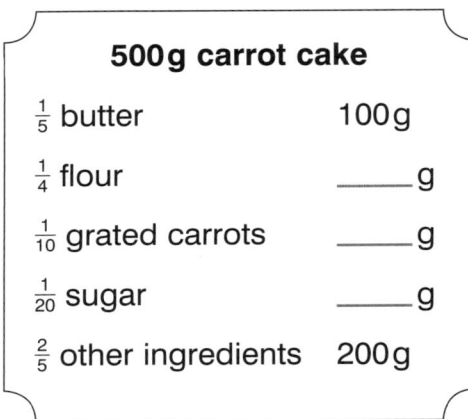

10 Write the weight of each ingredient in the recipe.

11 Using this recipe, how many grams of butter would be needed for an 800 g cake? _____

12 What fraction of £2 is each of these amounts?

10p _____   40p _____   £1.50 _____

Now go to the Progress Chart to record your score!   Total   12

Focus test 5 — Special numbers and number sequences

> A sequence is a list of numbers in a pattern. To find missing numbers look at the difference between the numbers.

1 What is the next number in this sequence?

   37   22   7   −8   −23   ____

Write the missing numbers in these sequences.

2 248   ____   ____   98   48   −2   ____

3 ____   −2.8   −1.9   ____   −0.1   ____   1.7

4 ____   9   16   25   36   ____   ____

What is the difference in temperature between each pair of thermometers?

5 _____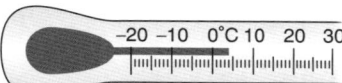

6 _____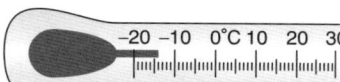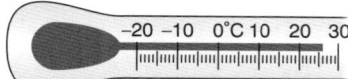

7 Which two square numbers total 100? ____ and ____

8 In this sequence you add the same amount each time. Write the missing numbers.

   5   ____   ____   ____   21

9 Will the number 41 be in this sequence? Circle the answer: yes   no

   −9   −4   1   6   11   …

10 Each number is double the previous number. Write the missing numbers.

    7   14   28   ____   ____   ____

11 What is 12^2? ____

12 What is the square root of 16? ____

Now go to the Progress Chart to record your score!   Total ⬭ 12

Focus test 6 — Equations and algebra

Josh made this shape pattern with counters.

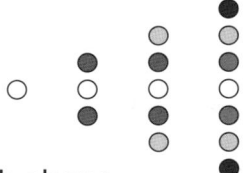

The table shows the number of counters he used for each shape.

Shape number	1	2	3	4	n
Counters	1	3	5	7	?

1 What is the correct formula for this dot pattern? Circle the answer.

$3n - 3$ $n + 1$ $4n - 5$ $2n - 1$ $n + 2$

2 How many counters would there be for the 20th shape pattern? _____

Work out the value of each symbol or letter.

3 □ + 4 = 19   □ = _____

4 ▲ − 5 = 13   ▲ = _____

5 $4y = 24$ $y = $ _____

6 $\dfrac{x}{3} = 15$ $x = $ _____

7 2∆ + 3 = 17   ∆ = _____

8 3▼ − 2 = 22   ▼ = _____

9 $2n - 8 = 30$ $n = $ _____

10 $14 - 2y = 4$ $y = $ _____

Equations use symbols or letters for unknown numbers in a calculation.

11 Is this statement 'true' or 'false'? Circle the answer.

If l is the length of a rectangle and w is the width of the rectangle, the formula $2(l + w)$ gives the perimeter of the rectangle.

true   false

12 Find the value of the following expressions if $x = 15$

$(28 - x) + 8 = $ _____ $3x - (8 \times 5) = $ _____ $(9 + 2x) - 8 = $ _____

Total 12

Focus test 7 — Shapes and angles

Look for the properties of 2-D shapes, including length of sides, any parallel lines, angle sizes and lines of symmetry.

1 Write the letter for each of these shapes in the correct part of the Carroll diagram.

	Pentagon	Not a pentagon
1 or more lines of symmetry		
No lines of symmetry		

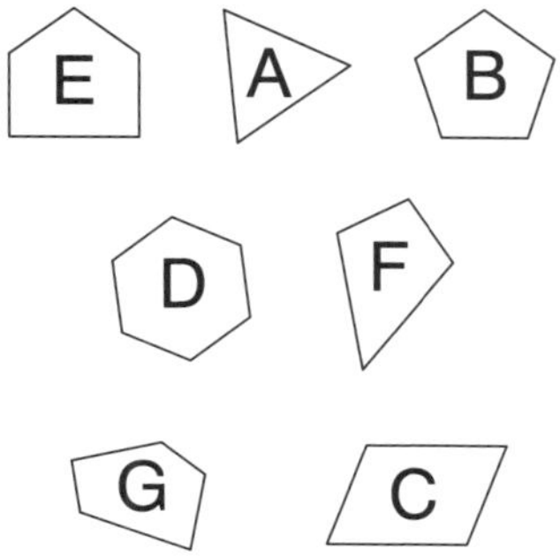

This is the net of a tetrahedron.

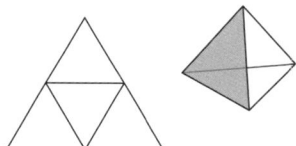

Write the name of each of these shapes from its net.

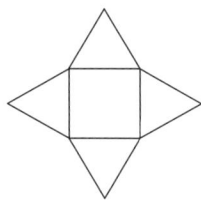

2 _____   3 _____

Two angles of this quadrilateral are 95° and 72°.

Measure the other two angles accurately using a protractor.

4 a = _____   5 b = _____

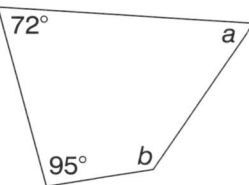

6 Here is part of a shape. Draw three more straight lines to make a shape with two lines of symmetry. Use a ruler.

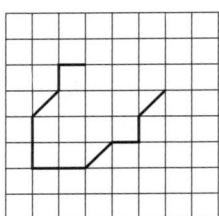

Rectangle ABCD has a diagonal line BC. Calculate the size of angles x and y.

7 angle x = ____

8 angle y = ____

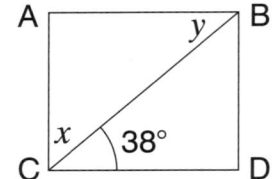

9 Is this statement 'always true', 'sometimes true' or 'never true'? Circle the answer.

An isosceles triangle has an obtuse angle.

always true   sometimes true   never true

AB and CD are parallel lines.

10 Which line is perpendicular to AB? ____

11 What is the angle z? ____

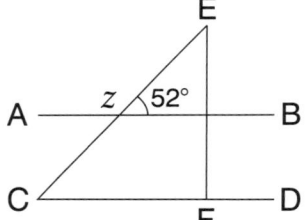

12 Look at this equilateral triangle inside a rectangle.

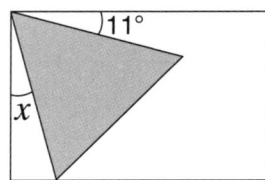

Calculate the value of x without using a protractor. ____

Now go to the Progress Chart to record your score!   Total   12

Focus test 8 — Area, perimeter and volume

Remember: Perimeter is measured in units such as centimetres (cm) and metres (m). Area is measured in square units such as cm^2 and m^2. Volume is measured in cubic units such as cm^3 and m^3.

Calculate the area and perimeter of this room.

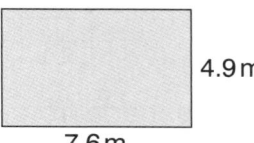

1 Area = _____

2 Perimeter = _____

3 What is the area of this triangle?

   Area of triangle = _____

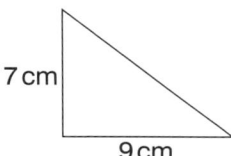

4 This star is made from a square and four triangles. What is the total area of the star?

   _____

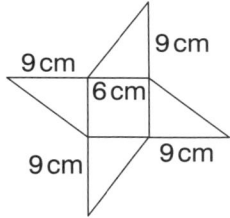

5 What is the area of this garden, not including the pond?

   _____

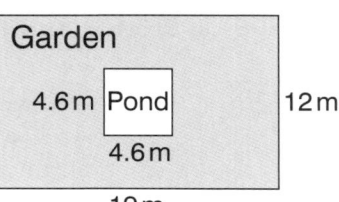

6 What is the area of this shape?

   _____

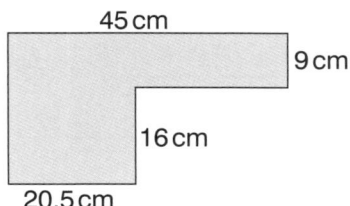

7 A cuboid has a square base with sides of 12 cm.
The volume of the cuboid is 1152 cm³.

What is the height of the cuboid? _____

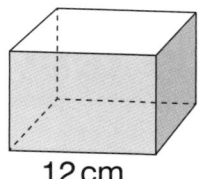
12 cm

8 On the grid draw a triangle with the same area as the rectangle.
Use a ruler.

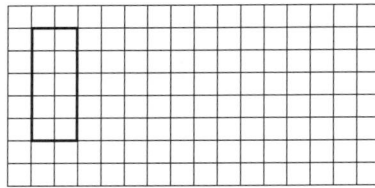

9 This shape is made from equilateral triangles and a square.
The square has sides of 21 cm.

What is the perimeter of the shape?

_____

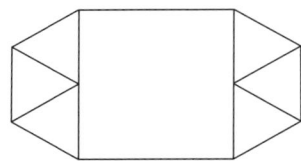

10 A square has sides of 105 mm.

What is the area of the square in square centimetres? _____

What is the perimeter of the square in centimetres? _____

11 A square has an area of 841 cm².

What is the length of each side? _____

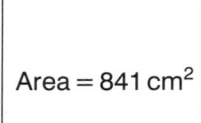
Area = 841 cm²

12 Calculate the difference in area of these two rooms.

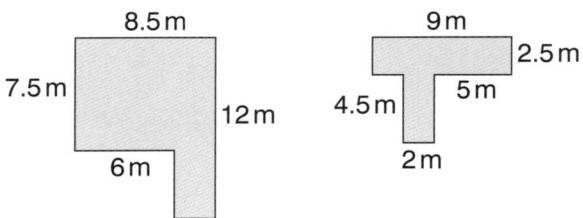

Area = _____   Area = _____

Difference = _____

Now go to the Progress Chart to record your score!   Total ( ) 12

Focus test 9 — Measures

We still sometimes use imperial units such as pints, feet and pounds. These are measures that were used in the past. Try to learn their approximate metric values.

Write the amount shown on each scale.

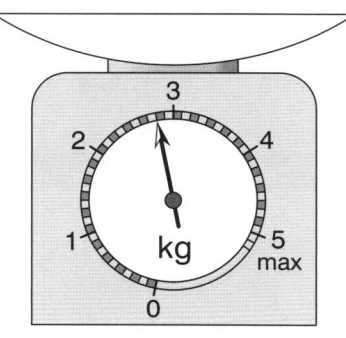

1 _____

2 _____

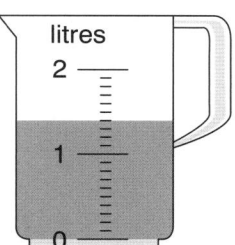

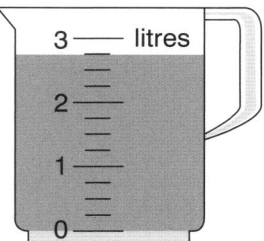

3 _____

4 _____

Complete these conversions.

5 675 mm = _____ cm

6 0.95 litres = _____ ml

7 84.8 m = _____ cm

8 3825 g = _____ kg

9 What is the length of this line in millimetres? _____

10 An athlete runs 15 laps of a 400 metre track. She wants to run a total of 10 km.

How many more laps does she need to run? _____

Circle the closest approximation for these imperial to metric conversions.

11 A tree is 20 feet tall. Approximately how many metres is this?

      0.6 m   60 m   6 m   3 m   10 m

12 Approximately how many miles are there in 160 km?

    20 miles   100 miles   150 miles   300 miles   80 miles

Now go to the Progress Chart to record your score!   Total   12

Focus test 10 — Transformations and coordinates

Coordinates are useful for showing an exact position of a point on a grid or for plotting the vertices of shapes. Remember to read the numbers on the horizontal x-axis first, then the vertical y-axis.

Do these shapes show a translation, rotation or reflection? Circle each answer.

1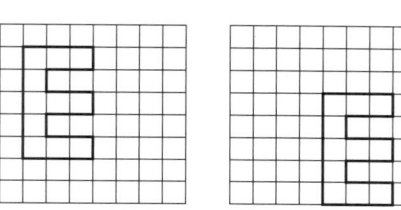

translation   rotation   reflection

2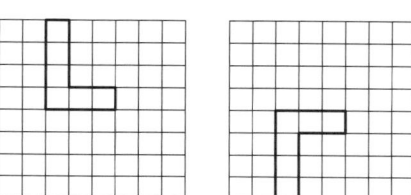

translation   rotation   reflection

3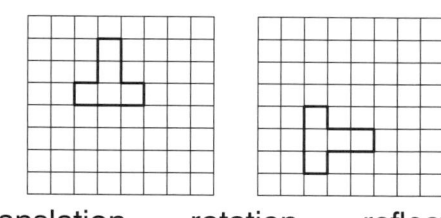

translation   rotation   reflection

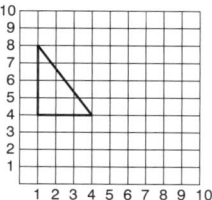

4 On the grid, draw another triangle at the coordinates: (9, 2), (6, 2) and (6, 6).

5 Is this triangle a translation, rotation or reflection of the first triangle?

_____

Here are two sides of a square.

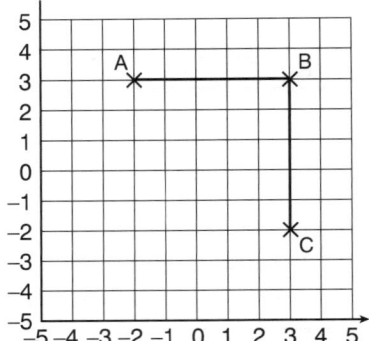

6 What are the coordinates of the three vertices?

A (__, __) B (__, __) C (__, __)

7 Mark the missing coordinates for the fourth vertex and complete the square.

8 What are the coordinates of the fourth vertex of the square? D (__, __)

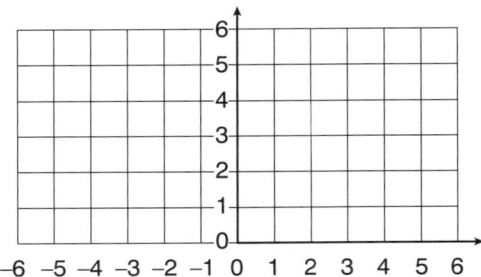

9 Plot these points on the grid and join them in order with a pencil and ruler.

(4, 1), (6, 4), (2, 4), (0, 1)

10 Reflect your drawing into the second quadrant and plot the points.

What are the coordinates of your shape?

(__, __) (__, __) (__, __) (__, __)

11 Colour squares on this grid to reflect this shape in the mirror line.

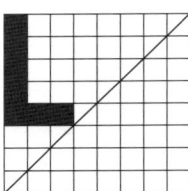

12 This is an isosceles triangle. Write in the missing coordinates.

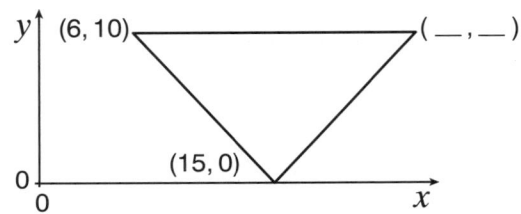

Now go to the Progress Chart to record your score!   Total   12

Focus test 11 — Charts, graphs and tables

Take a moment to read each graph so that you understand them before answering the questions.

This pie chart shows the number of goals scored by the top 5 players at a hockey tournament. These 5 players scored a total of **90 goals** between them.

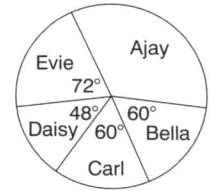

Goals scored by top 5 scorers

1 How many goals did the highest scorer get? _____

2 What fraction of the goals did Carl score? _____

3 What percentage of the goals did Evie score? _____

This frequency chart shows the number of goals scored by all the players in the hockey tournament.

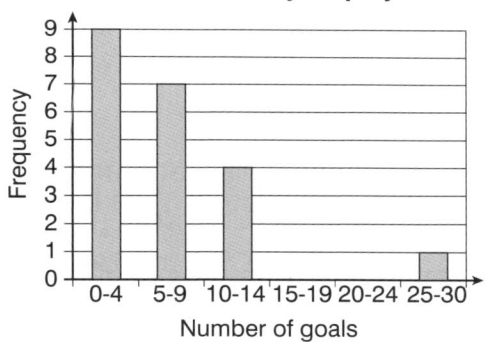

Goals scored by all players

4 How many players scored 5 or more goals but fewer than 10 goals?
_____

5 How many players altogether scored fewer than 10 goals? _____

6 Is this statement 'true', 'false' or is it 'impossible to say'? Circle the answer.

   Three players did not score a goal.

   true   false   impossible to say

This graph shows the number of goals scored each minute in all 6 games of hockey in the tournament.

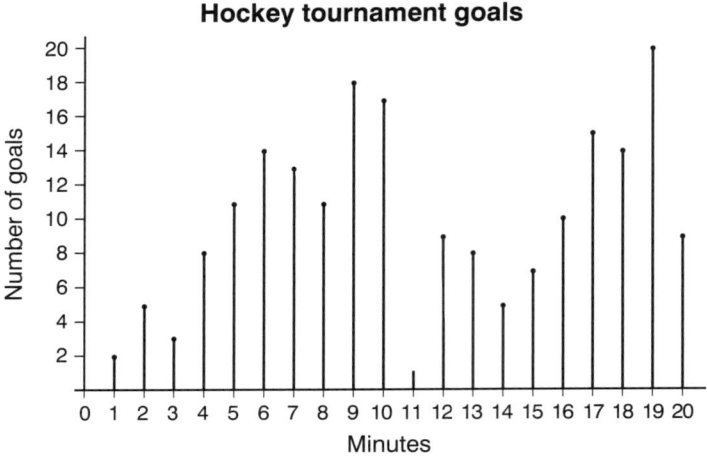

Hockey tournament goals

7 How many goals were scored in the first 5 minutes? _____

8 In which 3 minutes were the most goals scored? Circle the answer.

      8th–10th minutes   17th–19th minutes

9 In one particular minute the same number of goals was scored in all 6 games. How many goals were scored in each game in that one minute? _____

Look at **all** the graphs and charts and answer these questions. You need to decide which information is helpful for each task.

10 The goals of Evie, Carl and Bella are missing from the frequency chart. Look at the pie chart and use this information to complete the frequency chart.

11 There were 4 teams in the tournament. Use the completed frequency chart to work out how many players there were in each team _____

12 Is this statement 'true', 'false' or is it 'impossible to say'? Circle the answer.

Daisy scored one-third of her goals in the first minute.

      true   false   impossible to say

Now go to the Progress Chart to record your score!   Total 12

Focus test 12 — Mean, median, mode, range and probability

Number and price of ice creams sold

Flavour	vanilla	chocolate	cherry	lime	mint	peach	lemon
Number sold on Saturday	24	34	23	24	19	23	23
Number sold on Sunday	28	32	27	25	18	23	29
Price	£1.20	£1.55	£1.25	£1.40	£1.30	£1.35	£1.40

1. What is the mode number of ice creams sold on Saturday? _____
2. What is the mean number of ice creams sold on Sunday? _____
3. What is the median price of an ice cream? _____
4. Which day has the greatest range in the number of ice creams sold? _____

This information is about the number of ice creams of each flavour sold on Monday.

Range: 12

Lowest number sold of one flavour: 15

Mode: 20

Mean: 19

Flavour	vanilla	chocolate	cherry	lime	mint	peach	lemon
Number sold on Monday	27	20			15	20	18

5–6 Work out the two missing numbers for the ice creams sold on Monday.
_____ and _____

Remember: on a probability scale 0 is impossible, 1 is certain and the middle is 50/50 or an even chance.

This spinner has the numbers 1 to 6.

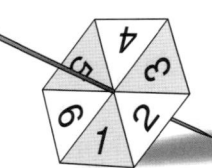

7 Draw an arrow on this probability scale to show the chance of spinning an odd number.

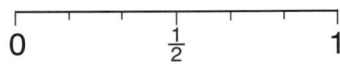

8 Draw an arrow on this probability scale to show the chance of spinning the number 3.

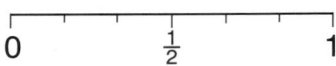

9 What is the chance of spinning a 7 on the spinner? Circle the answer.

$$0 \quad \tfrac{1}{2} \quad 1$$

These digit cards 1–9 are shuffled and placed face down.

10 What is the probability of picking an odd number from these digit cards? Circle the answer.

$$\tfrac{1}{2} \quad \tfrac{4}{9} \quad \tfrac{5}{9} \quad \tfrac{2}{3}$$

11 What is the probability (expressed in lowest term fraction) of picking a multiple of 3 from these digit cards? _____

12 Which of these is **more likely**? Circle the answer.

spinning a 2 on the spinner

picking a 2 from the set of digit cards

Now go to the Progress Chart to record your score!   Total   12

Mixed paper 1

1–3 Write 14 506 to the nearest 10, 100 and 1000.

14506	rounded to the nearest 10	_____
14506	rounded to the nearest 100	_____
14506	rounded to the nearest 1000	_____

4 I divide a number by 100. My answer is 84.7

What is the number? _____

5 Write < or > to make this statement true.

1.101 __ 1.011

6   409   **7**   196
        × 28   × 64

_____   _____

8 A mobile phone contract costs £13.50 each month. What is the total cost over a year? _____

9 (27 × 15) − 5 = _____

10 (33 × 26) + 2 = _____

11–14 What are the factors of 58? __, __, __ and __

15 Write the next prime number after 47. __

Fill in each space with one of these signs. < >

16 $\frac{3}{5}$ __ $\frac{7}{10}$

17 $\frac{5}{6}$ __ $\frac{2}{3}$

18 0.7 __ $\frac{3}{4}$

Write the missing digits to complete these.

19 $\dfrac{3}{\square} = 0.3 = \boxed{}\%$

20 $\dfrac{1}{\square} = 0.\boxed{} = 25\%$

Complete these sequences.

21–22   32   64   128   256   512   ____   ____

23–24   1   2   4   7   11   16   ____   ____

25 What is 49 written as a square number? ____

What number does each letter represent?

26 $6r + 4r = 70$ $r =$ ___

27 $8s - 3s = 90$ $s =$ ___

28 $36t \div 4 = 54$ $t =$ ___

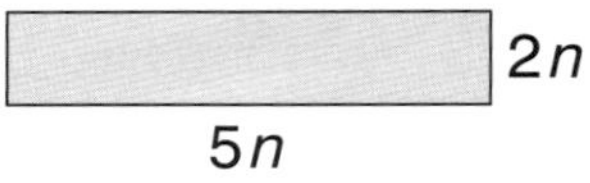

29 What is the **area** of this rectangle? ____

30 What is the **perimeter** of this rectangle? ____

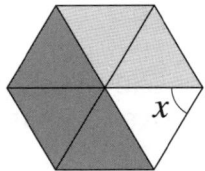

Look at this regular polygon.

31 What is the name of this whole shape? _____

32 How many lines of symmetry are there on this whole shape? ____

33 What is the name of the quadrilateral made from 3 triangles? _____

34 What is the name of the quadrilateral made from 2 triangles? _____

35 Calculate the size of angle x without using a protractor. ____

Calculate the area of these triangles.

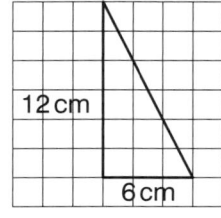   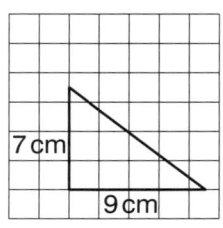   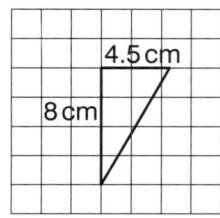

36 _____   37 _____   38 _____

A garden is a rectangular plot 7.8m long and 2.5m wide.

39 What is the area of the garden? _____

40 Fencing is sold in 1m lengths. How many 1m lengths of fencing would be needed to go all the way round the garden? _____

Fill in each space with one of these signs. <   >   =

41 0.8m ___ 75cm   **42** 2901g ___ 2.91kg

Look at these weights.

    12000g   2.01kg   12kg   2100g   20.1kg

43 Which weight is the heaviest? _____

44 Which two weights are the same? _____ and _____

45 A man is 6 feet tall. Circle the closest approximation in metric units.

    2000cm   20m   2m   200m   0.2m

A café sold 200 sandwiches. This pie chart shows the number of each type of filling.

Sandwich sales

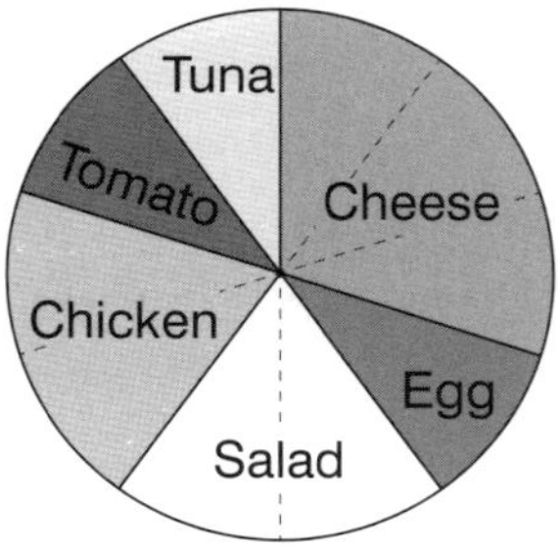

46 What percentage of sandwiches were filled with cheese? _____

47 How many chicken sandwiches were sold? _____

48 What fraction of the sandwiches were salad? Express the fraction in its lowest terms. _____

49 How many more cheese and tuna sandwiches were sold than tomato and chicken? _____

50 An extra 40 egg sandwiches were sold. Now, what percentage of the sandwiches were egg? _____

Now go to the Progress Chart to record your score! Total 50

Mixed paper 2

1. I am thinking of a number that has all three digits in consecutive order. It rounds to 3.5 to the nearest tenth.

   What is the number? ___ . ___ ___

2. Circle the smallest number.

   38.05   3.8   35.08   3.05   5.83   3.085

Write 10, 100 or 1000 to complete the first three calculations, and solve the others.

3. 230.7 ÷ _____ = 2.307

4. 59.041 × _____ = 590.41

5. 996.2 ÷ _____ = 0.9962

6. 572 × 13 = _____

7. 332 × 27 = _____

8. 287 × 32 = _____

9. There are 12 packs of paper in a box and 575 sheets of paper in each pack.

   How many sheets of paper are there in a box? _____

10. A driver travels a total of 29.5 km each day.

    How far does he travel in five days? _____

Write the numbers 7, 8 or 9 to complete these.

11–12 288 is a multiple of __ and __   13 312 is a multiple of __

14–15 441 is a multiple of __ and __

What fraction of 2m is each of these lengths?

16. 20 cm _____   17. 50 cm _____   18. 40 cm _____

19. 4.35 + 17.9 + 8.08 = _____   20. 30.66 + 0.25 + 1.39 = _____

21. Circle the square number in this set of numbers.

    46   48   24   64   86   44

Write the missing numbers in these sequences.

22–23 __   −21   −9   __   15   27

24–25 8   __   −4   −10   __   −22

26 What is the difference between −13 and 5? ___

The T-shapes in this sequence are made with interlocking cubes.

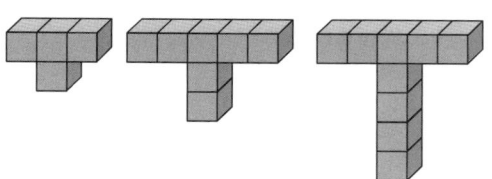

This table shows the number of cubes used for each shape.

Shape number	1	2	3	4	n
Cubes	4	7	10	___	?

27 How many cubes are needed for the 4th shape in this sequence? Write your answer in the table.

28 What is the correct formula for this T-shape sequence? Circle the answer.

$n + 3$ $4n - 1$ $3n + 1$ $n + 4$ $2n - 3$

29 How many cubes will there be in the 10th shape? ___

30–31 Underline the two equations that give the same answer.

$(a + b) \times c$ $ab + c$ $a(b + c)$ $(a \times b) + c$ $a + (b \times c)$

Name each angle. Choose from **acute**, **obtuse**, **reflex**, or **right angle.**

32 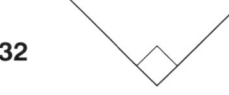 _____   **33** _____

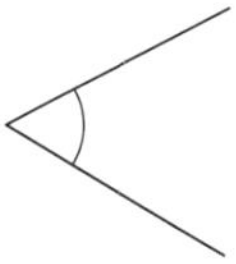

34  _____   **35**  _____

36 Write **always**, **sometimes** or **never** to make this sentence true.

An isosceles triangles _____ has a right-angle.

Measure each line to the nearest 5 mm. Use a ruler.

37 ━━━━━━━━━━━━━━━━━━━━━━━━━━━━━ ___ mm

38 ━━━━━━━━━━━━━━━━━ ___ mm

39 What is the difference in length between these two lines? Write your answer in centimetres. _____

40 Circle the largest amount.

370 ml   3.07 litres   7300 ml   37 000 ml   7.3 litres

41 Circle the longer distance.   50 kilometres   50 miles

42–44 Translate this shape 2 squares down and 4 squares to the right.

Write the coordinates of the vertices of your translated shape.

(__, __) (__, __) (__, __)

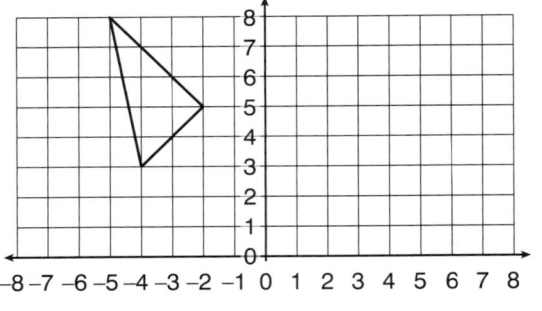

45 Is shape B a translation, rotation or reflection of shape A?

_____

46 Another shape has vertices at the coordinates (−2, −4) (0, −4) (0, −5) (2, −5) (2, −7) (−2, −7).

Is this shape a translation, rotation or reflection of shape A?

_____

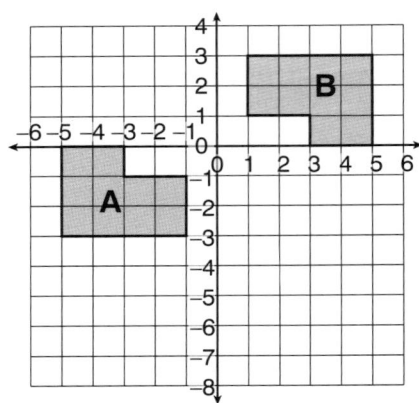

This graph shows the typical monthly temperatures in the UK.

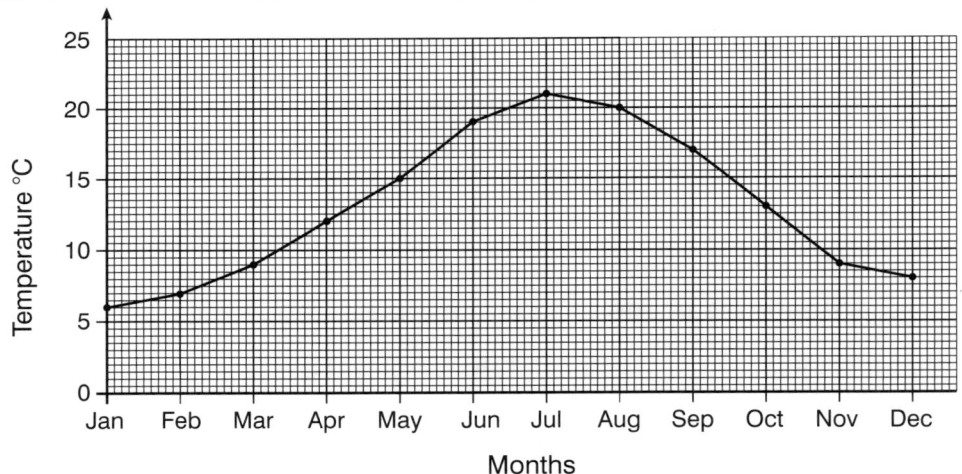

47 What is the mean temperature for the whole year? _____

48 What is the median temperature for the whole year? _____

49 What is the mode temperature? _____

50 What is the temperature range over the whole year? _____

Mixed paper 3

Complete these sequences.

1. 0.2   0.4   0.6   0.8   1   ____

2. 0.25   0.375 0.5   0.625 0.75   ____

3. 0.001 0.01   0.1   ____

4. What is the value of **7** in 36.704? ____

5. 9.28 × 1000 = ____

6. Four parcels each weigh 1.25 kg. What is the total weight of the four parcels? ____

7. A football tournament has 18 teams. Each team has 11 players and 2 substitutes. How many footballers in total will there be in the tournament? ____

8. A school buys 34 new computers costing £189 each. What is the total cost for these computers? ____

9. Jyoti multiplied a number by 8 instead of dividing a number by 8. Her answer was 3648. What should her answer have been? ____

10–12. Circle the numbers that are factors of 28.

   2   3   4   5   6   7   8   9

13. What number has these factors, 1 and itself? ____

   2, 3, 4, 6, 9, 12, 18

14–15. Circle the numbers that are **not** prime numbers.

   7   27   37   47   57

Change these fractions into decimals.

16. $\frac{34}{20}$ = ____   17. $\frac{9}{36}$ = ____

Change these survey results into percentages.

18. 37 out of 50 children preferred strawberry jam to raspberry jam. ____ %

19. 18 out of 25 bus passengers bought return tickets. ____ %

20. 8 out of 20 pet owners had a cat and a dog. ____ %

What is the difference in temperature between each pair of thermometers?

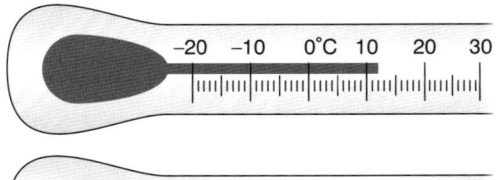
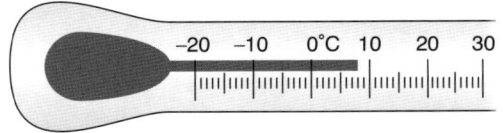
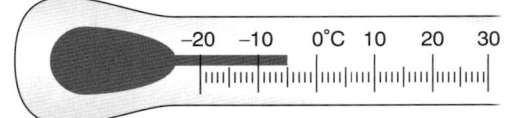
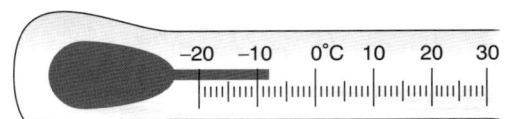

21 _____   22 _____

23–24 Write the missing numbers in this sequence.

36   49   64   81   ____   121   ____

Work out the value of each letter.

25 $8v - 31 = 1$ $v = $ ____

26 $3w + 9 = 27$ $w = $ ____

27 $5q - 12 = 19 + 4$ $q = $ ____

28 $8 + 7p = 6^2$ $p = $ ____

29 $\dfrac{r}{10} = 5.6 - 4.8$ $r = $ ____

30 A square has an area of 625 cm². What is the length of each side?
_____

31 Calculate the area of a square with a perimeter of 18 m.
_____

What is the area of these triangles?

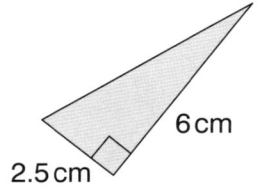
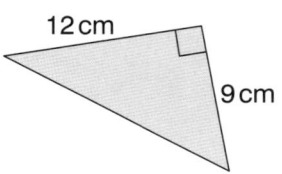

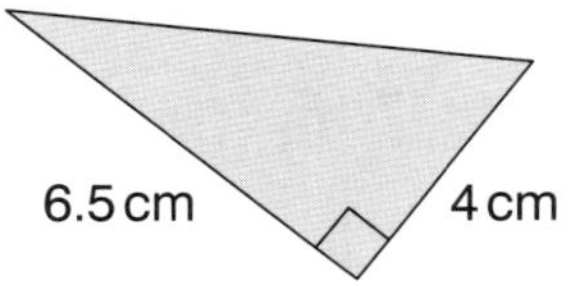

32 area = _____   33 area = _____   34 area = _____

35 A rug is 0.7 m wide and 2.3 m long. What is the perimeter of this rug in centimetres? ____ cm

Circle the correct answer for each of these.

36 25% of 3 litres   1.25 litres   1500 ml   725 ml   0.75 litres

37 20% of 5.6 kg   1120 g   1.2 kg   11.2 kg   560 g

38 $\frac{3}{4}$ of 8.4 km   2.1 km   3400 m   3.6 km   6300 m

Convert the weight shown on each of these scales to grams.

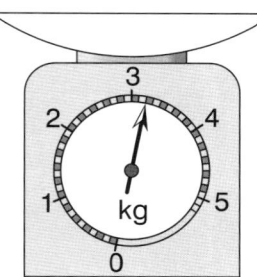

39 _____

40 _____

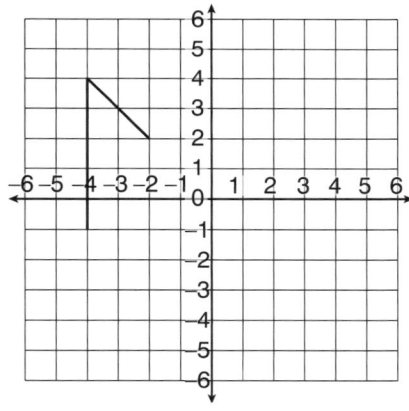

41 Mark the point (−2, −3) on the grid. This is the fourth corner of a quadrilateral. Draw two lines to complete this shape.

42 What is the name of this shape? _____

43–45 Rotate this shape 90° **clockwise** about the point (−2, −3). What are the coordinates of the other three corners of this rotated shape?

(−2, −3) (__, __) (__, __) (__, __)

A teacher asked the class to sort a box of shapes. The children recorded the number of each shape on this bar graph.

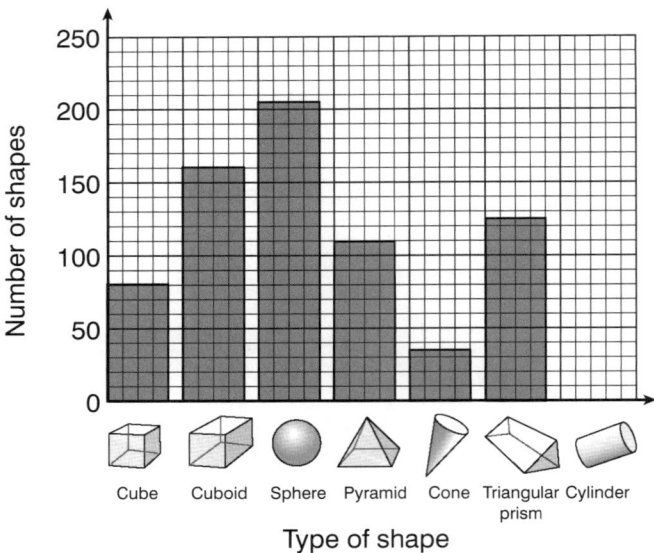

46 The children counted 85 cylinders. Accurately draw this bar on the graph.

47 Are there more shapes with 5 faces or 6 faces? _____

48 What is the difference between the number of cones and the number of spheres? _____

49 What percentage of the shapes are cuboids? _____

50 The teacher asked for all the shapes with a curved edge to be put into one box. How many shapes will there be in this box? _____

Mixed paper 4

What is the value of the **5** in each of these numbers?

1 58930 _____

2 0.652 _____

3 115.49 _____

4 7.588 _____

5 Multiply 33.764 by 10. _____

Solve these money problems and round your answers to the nearest whole pound.

6–7 £9.70 × 17 = _____ which is _____ to the nearest pound.

8–9 £6.57 × 13 = _____ which is _____ to the nearest pound.

10
$$\begin{array}{r} 288 \\ \times\ 31 \\ \hline \end{array}$$

_____

Choose from the numbers 3, 5, 7 or 8 to complete these statements.

11–12 5166 is a multiple of _____ and _____.

13–14 2560 is a multiple of _____ and _____.

Ali, Kim and Dan each have a skipping rope. Dan's skipping rope is half the length of Kim's. Ali's skipping rope is $1\frac{1}{2}$ times longer than Kim's. The total length of their ropes when placed in a line end to end is 6m.

15 What is the length of Ali's skipping rope? _____

16 What is the length of Dan's skipping rope? _____

17 What is the length of Kim's skipping rope? _____

Convert these **improper fractions** to **mixed numbers** in their **lowest terms**.

18 $\frac{30}{9}$ _____   19 $\frac{48}{10}$ _____

20 $10^2 - 4^2 =$ _____   21 $12^2 - 5^2 =$ _____

The rule for this sequence of numbers is: − 200

                     4049   3849   3649   3449

What is the rule for each of these sequences?

22   −46   −30   −14   2   18   rule: _____

23   30 000   27 500   25 000   22 500   rule: _____

24   6.4   4.2   2   −0.2   −2.4   rule: _____

25   $\frac{1}{2}$ $\frac{5}{8}$ $\frac{3}{4}$ $\frac{7}{8}$ 1   rule: _____

26–27 Work out the values of x and y in these triangles.

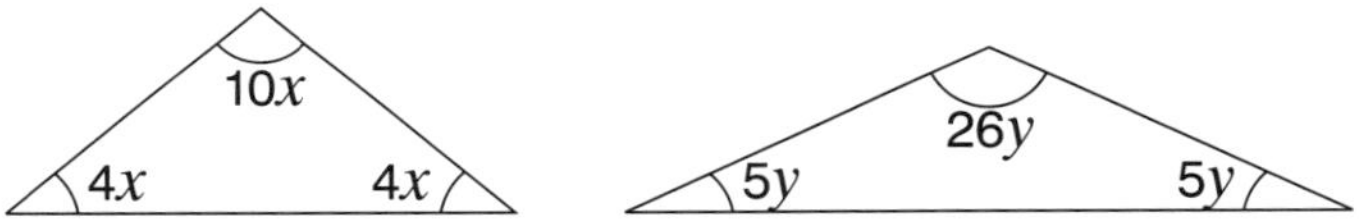

     (triangle with 10x at top, 4x and 4x at base)   (triangle with 26y at top, 5y and 5y at base)

$x =$ _____ $y =$ _____

28   $\sqrt{d} = 12$ What is the value of d? _____

29   $\frac{r}{2} = 3$ What is the value of r? _____

Look at this clock face and calculate the size of these angles. Do not use a protractor.

30 What is the size of the smaller angle between 12 and 4? _____

31 What is the size of the smaller angle between 8 and 9? _____

32 What is the angle between 5 and 11? _____

33 If the clock-hand is pointing to 1 and moves 90° clockwise, what number will it be pointing to now? _____

Calculate the area of these triangles. Scale: each square represents 1 cm²

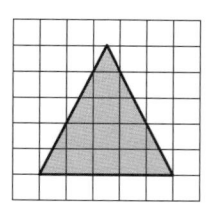

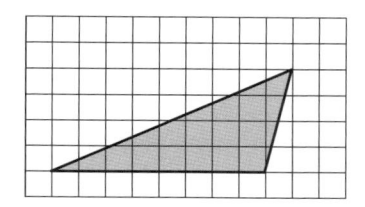

34 area = _____   **35** area = _____

36 These are the dimensions of a cupboard.

What is the volume of the cupboard?

volume = _____

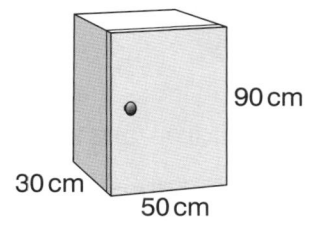

(90 cm, 30 cm, 50 cm)

This net will fold to make a cuboid with square ends.

37 Calculate the total surface area of the cuboid. _____

38 Calculate the volume of the cuboid. _____

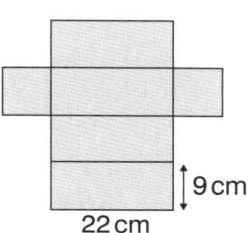

(9 cm, 22 cm)

39–40 The perimeter of a rectangular piece of paper is 900 mm. The length is 1.5 times the width. What is the length and width of this piece of paper?

Write your answers in centimetres.

length = _____   width = _____

41–43 This biscuit recipe is out of an old cook book. Convert the ingredients from imperial units to metric units. Give your answers to the nearest 5 g.

Use the approximation: 1 oz ≈ 28 g

Ingredient	Imperial	Metric
flour	14 oz	_____
butter	7 oz	_____
sugar	6 oz	_____

44 This recipe makes a total of eight biscuits. What is the weight of one biscuit? Give your answer in grams. _____

Children from three classes recorded the number of pets owned. They displayed the data on these pie charts.

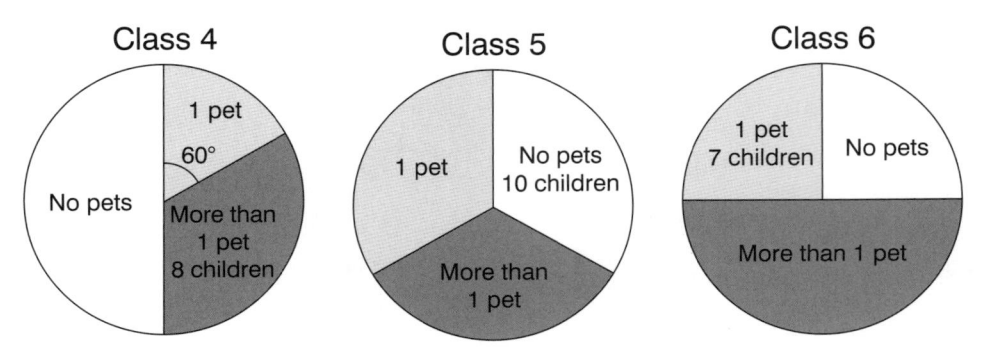

Class 4
- 1 pet 60°
- No pets
- More than 1 pet — 8 children

Class 5
- 1 pet
- No pets — 10 children
- More than 1 pet

Class 6
- 1 pet — 7 children
- No pets
- More than 1 pet

45–47 How many children are there in each class?

Class 4 _____ children

Class 5 _____ children

Class 6 _____ children

48 How many children in total from all three classes have only one pet? _____

49 How many more children have no pets in Class 4 than those with no pets in Class 6? _____

50 Is this statement 'true', 'false' or is it 'impossible to say'? Circle the answer.

The same number of children in Class 4 and Class 5 have more than one pet.

true   false   impossible to say

6

Now go to the Progress Chart to record your score!   Total   50

Mixed paper 5

Write these numbers on the answer lines to make this statement true.

2.09   0.927   0.279   2.7

1–4 ____ < ____ < ____ < ____

5 I'm thinking of a number less than 1. The two digits total 9 and it rounds to 0.4 to the nearest tenth.

What is the number I am thinking of? 0. __ __

6 A piece of wood is 189 cm long. It is cut into six equal lengths.

How long is each length? _____

7 (378 ÷ 18) + 19 = ____   8 (403 ÷ 13) + 15 = ____

9 A 2 litre bottle of lemonade is poured into 0.4 litre glasses.

How many glasses will be filled? ____

10 Joe saves the same amount each week. After 20 weeks he has saved £75.

How much does he save each week? _____

Circle the number in each row that has each pair of numbers as factors.

11 4 and 7   8   14   27   28   32

12 13 and 3   9   19   31   33   39

13 Circle the number that has five factors.

12   14   16   18

14–15 Two of these numbers are multiples of 4, 7 and 9. Circle them.

588   126   756   252   576

16 What is the ratio of round beads to square beads on this necklace?
_____

17 A longer necklace is made with the same pattern. If 15 round beads are used, how many square beads will be needed? ____

Change these fractions into decimals.

18 $\frac{24}{30}$ = _____   19 $\frac{28}{70}$ = _____

20 In a sale a coat is reduced by 40% from the original price of £125.

What is the new price of the coat in the sale? _____

21–22 Circle the two numbers that have a difference of 15.

−8   −6   −3   1   4   6   9

23 What is the square root of 81? _____

Leroy has made this pattern from colouring in squares on a grid.
The table shows the number of squares he coloured each time.

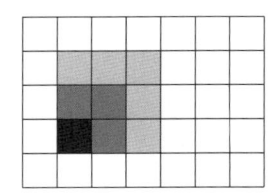

Shape	1	2	3	4	n
Squares	1	3	5	___	?

24 How many squares will he colour for the 4th shape? Write your answer in the table.

25 What is the correct formula for this pattern? Circle the answer.

n + 3   4n − 1   3n + 1   n + 4   2n − 1

26 Leroy continues with this pattern. How many squares will he colour in the 8th shape? _____

What is the value of each of these letters?

27 17 + 8e = 73   e = _____

28 4f + (27 ÷ 9) = 35   f = _____

A clock has the big hand on 12 and the small hand moves clockwise. What time is it when the angle between the two hands has these values?

29 180° _____ o'clock   30 30° _____ o'clock   31 150° _____ o'clock

32 What is the area of a rectangular car park that is 8.4m wide and 15m long? _____

Calculate the area of these shapes.

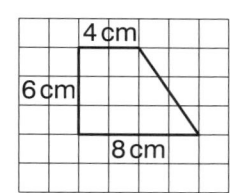

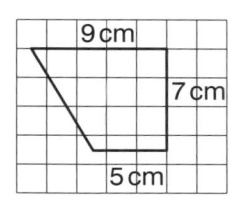

33 area = _____

34 area = _____

35 A cuboid has a square base of 36 cm². The volume of the cuboid is 5292 cm³.

What is the height of the cuboid? _____

Give each answer in the unit of measurement shown.

36 4738 m + 5.02 km _____ km

37 8.55 litres − 624 ml _____ litres

38 71.9 cm × 6 _____ m

39 1.93 kg − 1.074 kg _____ g

At the supermarket there are different size boxes of the same cereal.

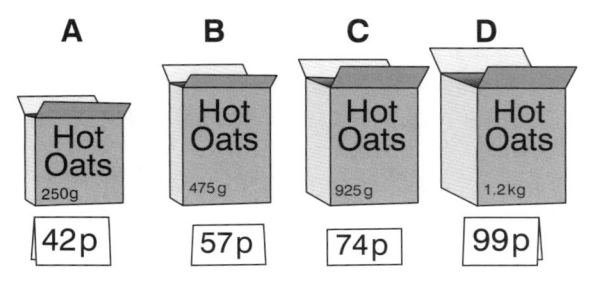

A Hot Oats 250g 42p

B Hot Oats 475g 57p

C Hot Oats 925g 74p

D Hot Oats 1.2kg 99p

40 Which box of cereal is the best value? _____

41 Which box of cereal is the least value? _____

42 Rotate line A 90° **clockwise** about the point (−4, −3). Draw the new line and label it B.

Complete the coordinates of line B.
(−4, −3) and (__, __)

43 Is line B **parallel** or **perpendicular** to Line A? _____

44 Lines A and B are two sides of a square.

What are the coordinates of the missing corner of this square? (__, __)

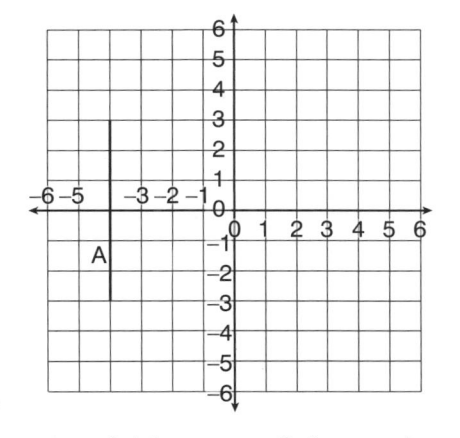

45 This is an isosceles triangle. Write in the missing coordinates.

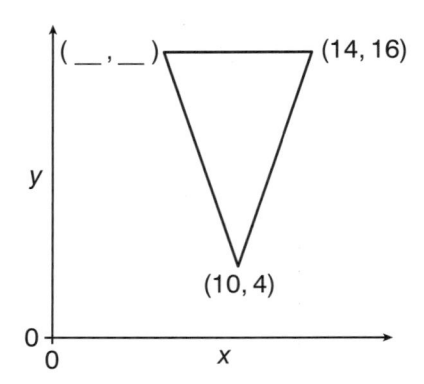

(_, _) at top-left; (14, 16) at top-right; (10, 4) at bottom.

These are the number of pages six children read in half an hour.

28   33   27   19   25   24

46 What is the range? _____   **47** What is the mean? _____

48 There is a $\frac{1}{5}$ chance of picking a raffle ticket that will win a prize. What is the probability of picking a raffle ticket that will not win a prize?
_____

There are 60 beads in a box, 12 are red, 18 are blue, 20 are green and the rest are yellow.

49 What is the chance of taking out a bead that is not yellow? Circle the answer.

$\frac{1}{2}$ $\frac{2}{3}$ $\frac{3}{4}$ $\frac{5}{6}$ $\frac{11}{12}$

50 What is the chance of taking out a blue bead? Circle the answer.

$\frac{1}{3}$ $\frac{3}{10}$ $\frac{3}{6}$ $\frac{1}{10}$ $\frac{3}{4}$

Now go to the Progress Chart to record your score!   Total   50

Mixed paper 6

Write the missing sign: × or ÷

1. 14.25 ___ 10 = 142.5

2. 0.587 ___ 100 = 58.7

3. 6.03 ___ 10 = 0.603

4. Round 29.648 to the nearest tenth. _____

5. Write in figures: six hundred and fifty-two thousand seven hundred and three. _____

6. 6 ÷ 0.4 = ____

7. 7.2 ÷ 8 = ____

8. 3.78 ÷ 6 = ____

9. 604
    ×26
    _____

10. 590
    ×17
    _____

11. Write **always**, **sometimes** or **never** to make this statement true.

    A square number _____ has an odd number of factors.

Look at this set of numbers.

80   81   82   83   84   85

12. Which is a prime number? ____ 13. Which is a square number? ____

14. Which is a multiple of 2 and 3? ____

15. A model village is made to a scale of 2 cm to every 3 metres. A real tree is 12 m tall.

    What is the height of the model tree? _____

Circle the smallest value in each set.

16. $\frac{5}{8}$ of 24 $\frac{2}{3}$ of 18 $\frac{2}{5}$ of 25 $\frac{3}{7}$ of 21

17. 0.27   0.07   0.2   0.72

18. $\frac{40}{56}$ $\frac{8}{14}$ $\frac{27}{63}$ $\frac{42}{49}$

19 Write < or > to make this statement true.   2% __ 0.2

20 $6^2 + 3^2 =$ _____

21 What is 20 more than −7? _____

22 $\sqrt{100} + 33 =$ _____

23 Which two square numbers total 80? _____ and _____

24 Circle the formula for the **area** of this triangle.

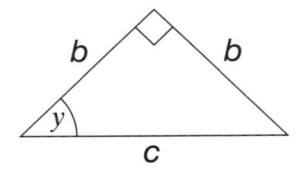

2(b × c)   (b × b) ÷ 2   2(b × b)   (2 × c) ÷ b

25 Circle the formula for the **perimeter** of this triangle.

b + c   2b − c   b − c   2b + c   2b + 2c

26 Circle the name of this type of triangle.

isosceles   equilateral   scalene

27 Calculate the size of angle *y* in this triangle. _____

28 Draw one line of symmetry on this triangle.

29–32 Write the missing information in this table.

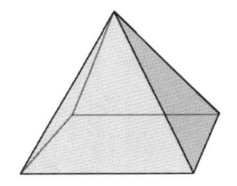

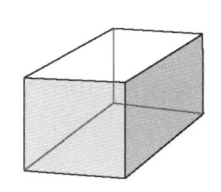

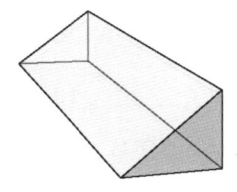

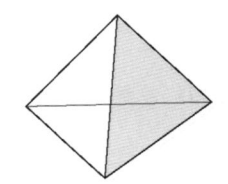

Shape name	Number of faces	Number of corners	Number of edges
tetrahedron	—	4	6
cuboid	6	8	—
square-based pyramid	5	—	8
triangular prism	5	6	—

33 Which net will **not** fold to make a closed cube? _____

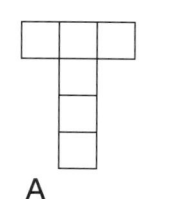

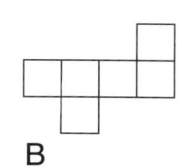

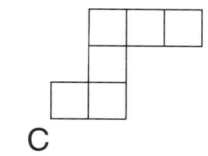

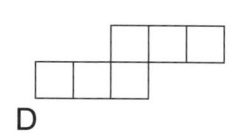

A   B   C   D

34 Draw three more lines to make a parallelogram with an area of 12 squares.

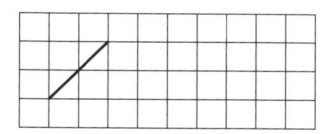

The top of this table has a surface area of 3200 cm². The length of the table-top is double the width.

35–36 What is the length and width of the table-top?

length = _____   width = _____

37 The tablecloth hangs over the edge of the table by 15 cm all the way round.

What is the area of the tablecloth? _____

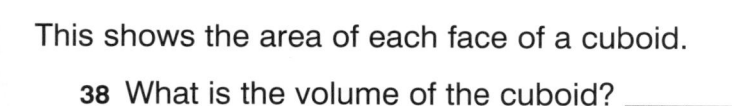

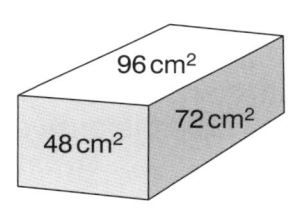

This shows the area of each face of a cuboid.

38 What is the volume of the cuboid? _____

96 cm²
72 cm²
48 cm²

39 Circle the name of this type of triangle.

equilateral   isosceles   scalene   right-angled

40 How many lines of symmetry are there on this triangle? _____

41–43 Draw another triangle using these coordinates: (0, 3), (2, 9) and (4, 3)

44 Is this triangle a translation, rotation or reflection of the first triangle?

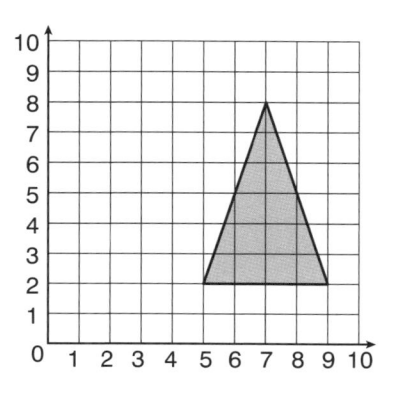

_____

45

Distance conversion (kilometres to miles)

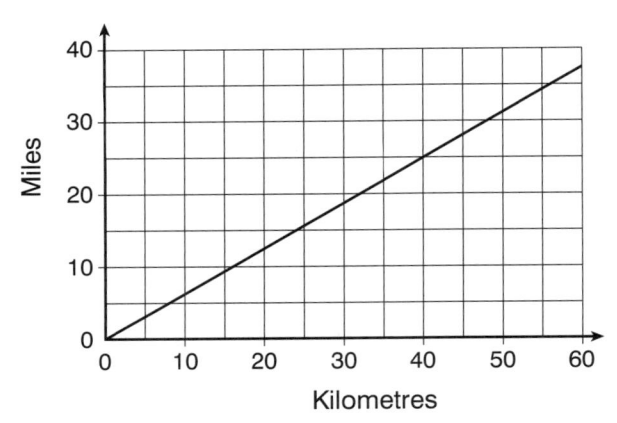

45–47 Use this conversion graph to convert these distances.

16 km: _____ miles (to the nearest whole mile)

28 miles: _____ kilometres (to the nearest whole km)

23 miles: _____ kilometres (to the nearest whole km)

48 Which is the further distance? 20 miles or 30 km _____

49 A lorry only has enough fuel to drive 15 miles. A sign shows that the filling station is in 22 km. Does the lorry have enough fuel to get to the filling station? Circle the answer.   Yes   No

50 The speed on my car is shown in miles per hour (mph). I am travelling in France and the speed limit is 50 km per hour (kph). What is the fastest speed I can drive my car and not go over the 50 kph speed limit? Give the answer to the nearest 10 mph. _____ mph

Now go to the Progress Chart to record your score!   Total   50

Mixed paper 7

Round each number to the nearest tenth.

1. 0.71 _____
2. 2.35 _____
3. 10.164 _____
4. 96.48 _____

5. A wall is 100 bricks high and each brick is 0.08m high.
   What is the height of the wall? _____

6. What is the product of 384 and 23? _____

7. Write the missing digits.

   103
   $45)\overline{4\_3\_}$

8. If six plates cost £8.40 how much would eight plates cost?
   _____

Give each answer in grams.

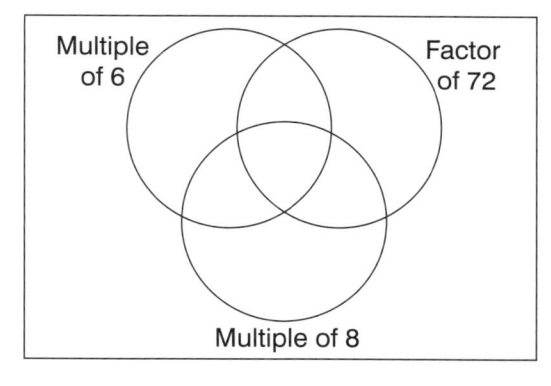

9. 1.82kg ÷ 7 = _____
10. 2.61kg ÷ 15 = _____

11–15 Write these numbers on the Venn diagram:

24   36   54   86   104

(Venn diagram with three circles labelled "Multiple of 6", "Factor of 72", and "Multiple of 8")

16. 4.35 + 17.9 + 8.08 = _____
17. 30.66 + 0.25 + 1.39 = _____

Change these fractions into percentages.

18. $\dfrac{24}{96}$ = _____
19. $\dfrac{45}{150}$ = _____

20. On a school watersports trip there must be a ratio of 2 adults to every 5 children. Class 4H has 32 children and Class 4K has 28 children.
    How many adults are needed? _____

21-22 Write the missing numbers.

$\_\_^2 + \_\_^2 = 5^2$

23 $9^2 - 2^2 = \_\_\_\_$

24 What is 24^2? ____

Use *l* for the length and *w* for width to answer these questions.

25 Circle the formula for the **perimeter** of this rectangle.

$4(w + l)$ $\frac{1}{2}(w + l)$ $2(w + l)$ $w(2 + l)$

26 This equation shows the area of a rectangle. Calculate the length, *l*, of the rectangle.

$345 \,cm^2 = l \times 15 \,cm$ $l = \_\_\_\_$

Write the value of each letter in these equations.

27 $4m^2 = 64$ $m = \_\_\_\_$

28 $3n^2 = 108$ $n = \_\_\_\_$

29 $o^2 = 90 - 41$ $o = \_\_\_\_$

Write the name of the solid shape that can be made from each net.

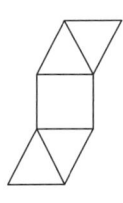

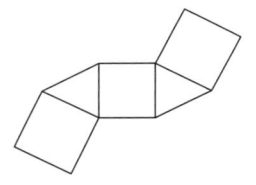

30 _____   **31** _____

32 The dashed line is a mirror line. Draw the reflected shape.

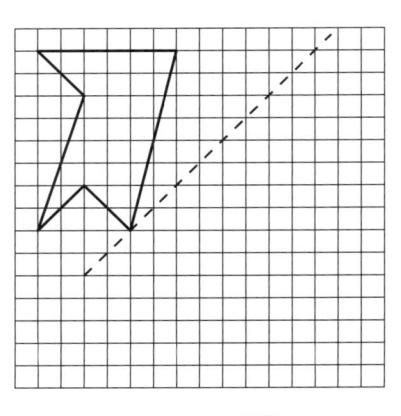

33–35 Calculate the angle marked with the letter in each shape.

Shape 1   Shape 2 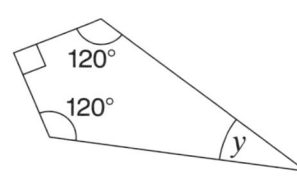   Shape 3

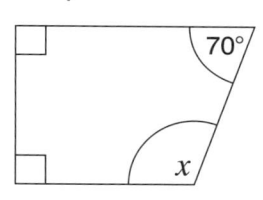

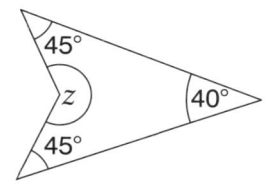

angle x = _____   angle y = _____   angle z = _____

36–39 Complete the following chart.

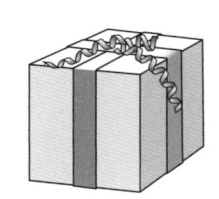

Gift box shape	Length of lid	Width of lid	Area of lid	Height of box	Volume of box
cube	_____	17cm	289cm²	17cm	_____
cuboid	9.5cm	8cm	_____	_____	8740cm³

40 Calculate the total area of this windmill. _____

18cm
15cm

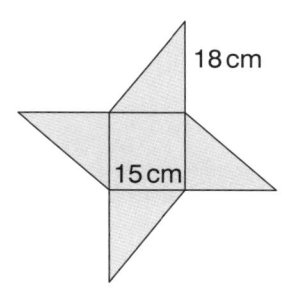

41 What must be added to 405g to make 1.56kg? Write your answer in kilograms. _____

42 Circle the longer length.

50cm   50 inches

Give each answer in the unit of measurement shown.

43 12.6kg ÷ 9 = _____ g

44 44m ÷ 8 = _____ cm

49

This graph shows the time it took two walkers to complete a 30 km walk.

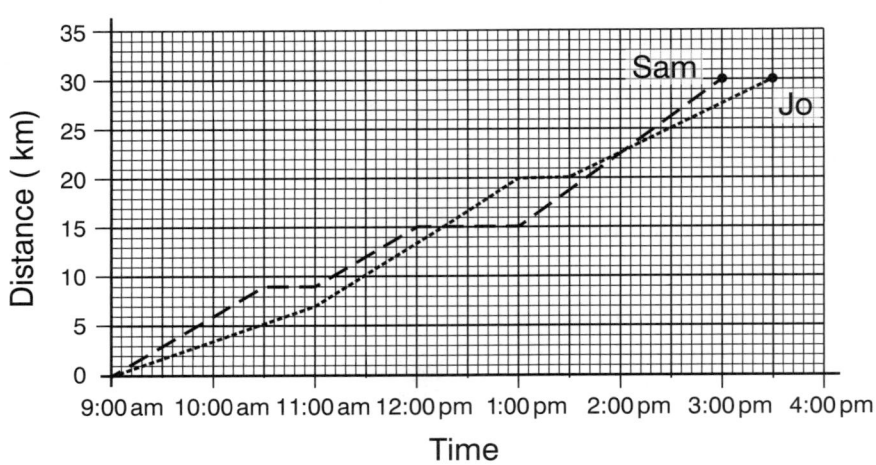

30 km sponsored walk

45 How far had Sam walked by 10:30 am? _____

46 Who finished their walk first, Sam or Jo? _____

47 How long did Sam stop for rests in total? _____

48 How much further had Sam walked than Jo at 11:00 am? _____

49 Sam was sitting eating lunch when Jo walked past. Approximately what time was this? _____

50 What was Jo's average speed for the 30 km walk, not including rest time? ____ km per hour

Mixed paper 8

Round each of these numbers to the nearest whole number.

1 491.3 ____   2 27.449 ____   3 50.52 ____

Convert each length to kilometres.

4 8806 m = ____   5 176 m = ____

6 A chicken farmer collects 760 eggs in one day. An egg carton holds 12 eggs.

How many full cartons will there be and how many eggs are left over?

____ full cartons   ____ eggs left over

7 By how much is the product of 15 and 29 greater than their sum? ____

8 7566 ÷ 26 = ____   9 2704 ÷ 32 = ____   10 5100 ÷ 17 = ____

11 What is the **highest common factor** of 18 and 45? ____

12–13 Circle the **prime factors** of 18.

2   3   4   5   6   7   8   9

14–15 5 is a **prime factor** of 315.

What are the other two prime factors? ____ and ____

Five biscuits are made from 75 g of flour, 50 g of butter and 25 g of sugar.

16 How much will each biscuit weigh? ____

17 What proportion of the biscuit is sugar? Circle the answer.

$\frac{1}{2}$ $\frac{1}{4}$ $\frac{1}{5}$ $\frac{1}{6}$

18 How much butter is needed if 300 g of flour is used? ____

19 What is the ratio of flour to butter in this recipe? Circle the answer.

1:1   2:1   3:2   6:1   7:5

Look at this set of numbers.

21   29   39   49   51

20 Which number is a square number? ____

21 Which number is a prime number? ____

22 The temperature on a thermometer at midday was 11°C. The thermometer was read again at midnight and the temperature had dropped by 14°C.

What was the temperature at midnight? _____

Write the next number in each sequence.

23 1   1   2   3   5   8   _____

24 36864   18432   9216   4608   _____

25 3000   300   30   3   _____

Use *l* for the length and *w* for width to answer these questions.

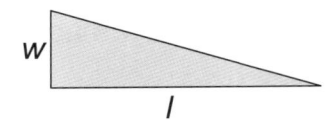

26 Circle the formula for the **area** of this triangle.

$2(l \times w)$ $(l \times w) \div 2$ $(l \times w) + 2$ $2(w \div l)$

27 Calculate the area of this triangle, when $w = 4$ cm and $l = 15$ cm. _____

If $s = 8$ and $t = 9$, what is the value of each of these equations?

28 $(7s - 11) \div t =$ _____

29 $t^2 - (s + 13) =$ _____

30 $16t \div s =$ _____

31 A shape has 5 faces, 6 corners and 9 edges.

What is the name of this shape? _____

32 The net of a shape has one pentagon and five triangles.

What is the name of this shape? _____

33 Name the solid shape that can be made from this net. _____

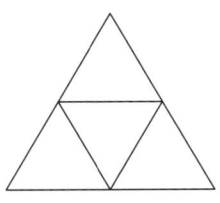

34 A regular hexagon has sides 14 mm long.

What is the perimeter of this hexagon in centimetres? _____ cm

35 Add together 585 ml, 3.2 litres and 1 litre 75 ml. Write your answer in litres. _____

36 Circle the greater length.   9 metres   9 feet

Give each answer in the unit of measurement shown.

37 470 cm + 3062 mm + 1.603 m = _____ mm

38 51 cm + 51 mm + 51 m = _____ cm

39 879 cm + 400 mm + 9.4 m = _____ m

40–43 Plot these coordinates and join them in order to make a quadrilateral. Label each point with its letter. Draw a line from point D to point A to complete the shape.

A (1, 3)   B (−2, 6)
C (−5, 3)   D (−2, −5)

44 What is the name of this shape? _____

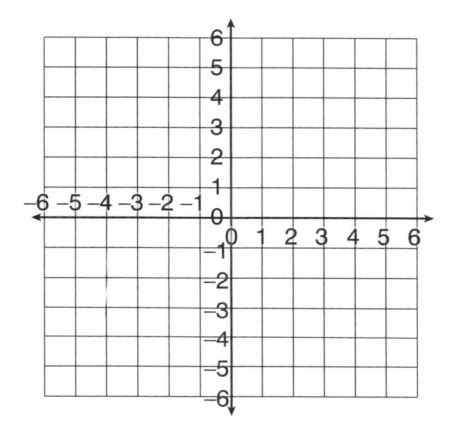

These 10 cards were placed in a bag and selected randomly.

| 10 | 20 | 30 | 40 | 50 | 60 | 70 | 80 | 90 | 100 |

For each question, write the probability as a decimal. Use this scale to help you.

Impossible   Certain
0   0.5   1

45 What is the probability of picking a number that is greater than 35? _____

46 What is the probability of picking a square number? _____

47 What is the probability of picking an odd number? _____

48 What is the probability of picking a multiple of 3? _____

49 What is the probability of picking an even number? _____

50 What is the probability of picking a multiple of 4? _____

Now go to the Progress Chart to record your score!   Total   50

Mixed paper 9

These are the times for the medallists in the women's 50m freestyle swimming final in the 2004 Olympics.

Swimmer	Time (seconds)
Libby Lenton, Australia	24.91
Inge De Bruijn, Netherlands	24.58
Malia Metella, France	24.89

1 What was the winning time?

__ __ . __ __ seconds

Divide each number by 100 to give the **quotient**.

2 703.16 _____   3 59.4 _____

Use these four digits and the decimal point to answer both questions.

[3] [8] [0] [5] [.]

4 What is the largest possible number? __ . __ __ __

5 What is the smallest possible number? __ . __ __ __

6 The product of two numbers is 1083. One of the numbers is 57.

What is the other number? _____

7 Which number, when multiplied by 45 will give the same answer as

7.2 × 100? _____

8 Five cinema tickets cost a total of £22.25. The tickets were all the same price.

How much was one ticket? _____

9–10 Write the missing digits in this calculation.

3__2 × 24 = 844__

11–14 Write these numbers on the Carroll diagram.   147   121   49   128

	Square number	Not a square number
Multiple of 7	_____	_____
Not a multiple of 7	_____	_____

Change these fractions into percentages.

15 $\dfrac{42}{210}$ = _____

16 $\dfrac{68}{80}$ = _____

Class 3 recorded the number of each type of vehicle passing the school.

Cars	Bikes	Lorries	Buses
144	36	48	12

17 What percentage of vehicles were cars? _____

18 What fraction of vehicles were lorries? Express the fraction in its lowest terms. _____

19 What percentage of vehicles were buses? _____

20 Out of the Bikes group, 27 were bicycles. What fraction of the Bikes group were bicycles? Express the fraction in its lowest terms. _____

21 Write < or > to make the following true. $\sqrt{36}$ __ 6.3

22–24 In this sequence the same amount is added each time. Write the missing numbers.

5   __   __   __   37

Write the value of each letter in these equations.

25 $\dfrac{j}{260} = \dfrac{3}{4}$ j = __

26 $\dfrac{k + 10.5}{60} = 20\%$ k = __

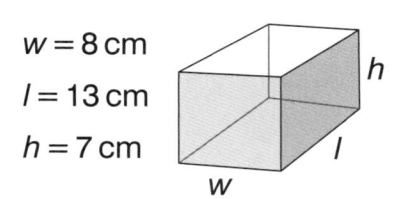

w = 8 cm
l = 13 cm
h = 7 cm

27 What is the name of this shape? _____

28 Calculate the volume of this shape. _____

55

Work out the value of the angles x, y and z in these triangles.

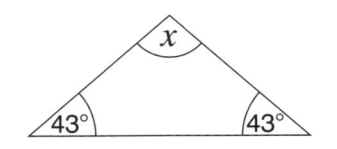

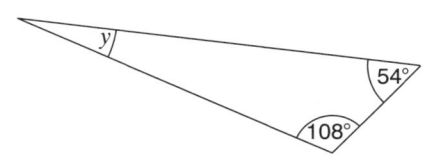

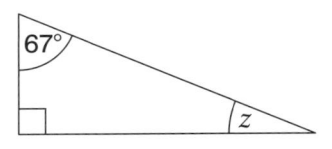

29 $x =$ _____ **30** $y =$ _____ **31** $z =$ _____

Look at this net. The length of one side of the square is 8 cm.

32 Which of these shapes can be made from this net? Circle your answer.

triangular prism   cube   tetrahedron   square-based pyramid

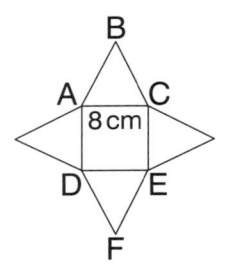

33 The area of each triangle is 32 cm². What is the total area of the net? _____

34 Which line is parallel to line DF? _____

35 Name a line that is perpendicular to line DE. _____

36 Is this statement true or false? _____

The angle at B is a right angle.

37 2 litres of paint will cover an area of 34 m².

What area can be covered by 500 ml of paint? _____

Circle the best answer for each of these questions.

38 A house is 25 feet tall. Approximately how many metres is this?

       0.8 m   4 m   80 m   8 m   40 m

39 The speed dial on a car is in 'miles per hour' (mph). In France the speed limit is given in 'kilometres per hour' (kph). The speed limit on a French road is 80 kph.

What speed in mph is closest to this?

       30 mph   40 mph   50 mph   60 mph

40 How many cups holding 350 ml can be filled from 4.2 litres of water? _____

41 The petrol tank on a lawnmower holds a maximum of 4.5 litres. The gauge shows there is 980 ml in the tank now. How much more petrol is needed to fill the tank? Write your answer in litres. _____

42–44 What are the coordinates of points A, B and C?

A (__, __)   B (__, __)   C (__, __)

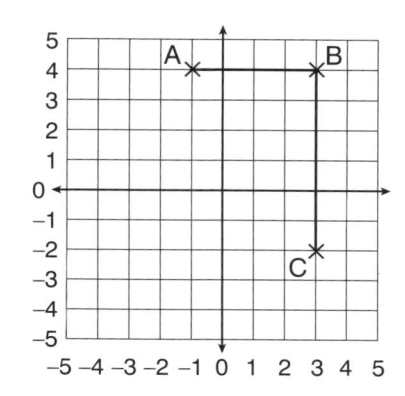

Lines AB and BC are two sides of a rectangle.

45 Mark the position of the fourth vertex and complete the rectangle.

46 What are the coordinates of the fourth vertex of the rectangle? (__, __)

These two pie charts show the number of days it rained in February and June. It was not a leap year.

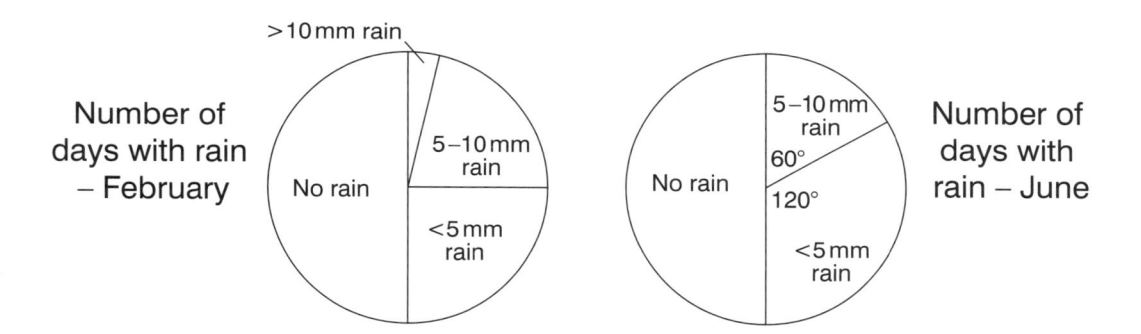

Number of days with rain – February

Number of days with rain – June

47 How many days in June had 5–10 mm of rain? ____

48 What fraction of the days in June had less than 5 mm rain? ____

49 What percentage of days in February had more than 5 mm of rain? ____

50 Is this statement 'true', 'false' or is it 'impossible to say'? Circle the answer.

Although half the days in both February and June had no rain, June had one more day with no rain than February.

true   false   impossible to say

Now go to the Progress Chart to record your score!   Total 50

Mixed paper 10

1. (42 ÷ 7) + 14.5   What is the answer divided by 100? _____
2. (11 × 24) + 6   What is the answer divided by 1000? _____
3. Round 6503g to the nearest kilogram. _____ kg
4. Write < or > to make the following true.   4.141 __ 4.411
5. Use these four digits and the decimal point to make the largest possible decimal number between 4 and 5.

   [3] [7] [5] [4] [.]

   __ . __ __ __

6. Three whole numbers multiplied together total 3240. Two of the numbers are 12 and 15. What is the third number? _____

7. 4)‾22.4

8. What is the next even number after 382 that 9 will divide into without a remainder? _____

9–10. Write the missing digits in this calculation.   486 × __5 = 7__90

11. What is the lowest common multiple of 10 and 12? _____

12. Write **always**, **sometimes** or **never** to make this statement true.

    A square number will _____ have an even number of factors.

13. Write the next number in this sequence of consecutive prime numbers.

    23   29   31   37   __

14. Which three prime numbers multiply to make 170? __, __, __

15–18. Put these values in order, starting with the smallest.

    $\frac{34}{85}$ 65% $\frac{42}{60}$ 0.46

    __ < __ < __ < __

There are three different flavoured sweets in a packet. There are 4 cherry to 3 lemon to 1 mint. There are 32 sweets in a pack. Calculate the number of each flavour sweet.

19 cherry: _____   **20** lemon: _____   **21** mint: _____

Write the next two numbers in each sequence.

22–23 −58   −45   −32   −19   ___   ___

24–25 16.8   12.6   8.4   4.2   ___   ___

What number does each letter represent?

26 $5g + 1 = 3.5$ $g = $ ___   **27** $\frac{h}{4} - 0.25 = 0.5$ $h = $ ___

28 $7p = 63$ $p = $ ___   **29** $(52 - 3r) \times 2 = 62$ $r = $ ___

30 $3(4a + 2a) = 90$ $a = $ ___

Look at these lines. Circle **true** or **false** for each statement.

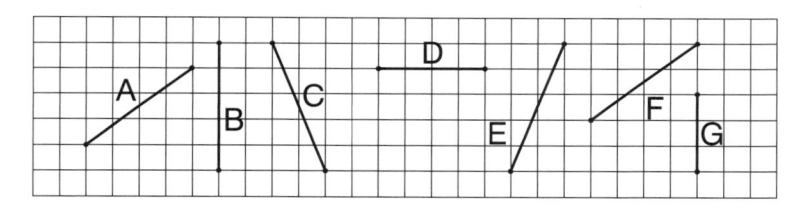

31 There is no line perpendicular to B.   **true   false**

32 There is no line parallel to E.   **true   false**

33 There are two lines perpendicular to D.   **true   false**

34 Lines A and F are parallel.   **true   false**

Look at this cuboid.

35 What is the area of face A? _____

36 What is the perimeter of face C? _____

37 What is the volume of the cuboid? _____

13.5 cm   45 cm   23 cm

38 In a market the apples are weighed in pounds. Circle the best approximate weight for 2 lb of apples.

10 kg   1000 g   100 kg   0.1 kg   100 g

39 Circle the greater capacity.   50 litres   50 pints

40 Eggs are put into a square tray that has 6 eggs in a row. There is an equal space between each egg in a row and between each row. The approximate weight of an egg is 62g and the tray itself weighs 18g.

What is the approximate weight in kilograms of a tray full of eggs? _____ kg

41 A runner completes a 5km race in 42 minutes. He runs at the same pace for the whole distance.

How many metres has he run after 10 minutes? Write your answer in kilometres to 2 decimal places. _____ km

42 A coolbox is 300mm high, 200mm wide and 400mm deep.

What is the volume of the coolbox in cubic centimetres? _____ cm^3

Reflect this rectangle into the second quadrant and plot the points.

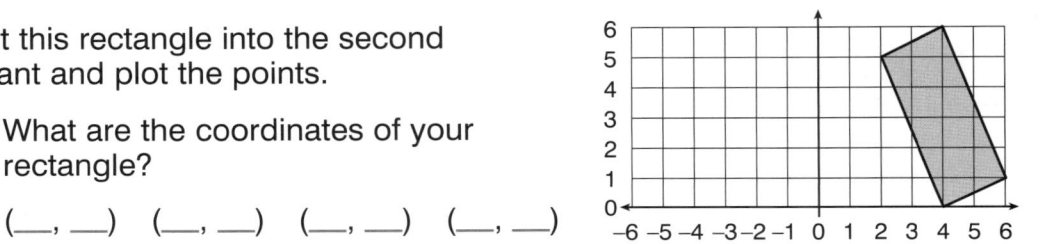

43–46 What are the coordinates of your rectangle?

(__, __) (__, __) (__, __) (__, __)

47 Five cards are chosen from two sets of 1–10 number cards. The median is 6, the mode is 7, the mean is 5 and the range is 5.

What are the two lowest numbers on the cards? __ and __

There are 4 apples, 5 pears and 3 oranges in a bag.

48 What is the probability of picking out an orange? Circle the answer.

$\frac{2}{3}$ $\frac{1}{2}$ $\frac{1}{3}$ $\frac{3}{4}$ $\frac{1}{4}$

49 What is the probability of picking out a pear? Circle the answer.

$\frac{5}{7}$ $\frac{1}{5}$ $\frac{4}{12}$ $\frac{5}{12}$ $\frac{1}{4}$

50 What is the probability of picking out a fruit that is not an apple? Circle the answer.

$\frac{2}{3}$ $\frac{1}{2}$ $\frac{4}{12}$ $\frac{3}{4}$ $\frac{7}{12}$

Now go to the Progress Chart to record your score!   Total   50